T0195828

Grades 3-6

# Thinking Through Analogies

Written by **Bonnie Lou Risby**
Illustrated by **Dean** and **Pat Crawford**

Routledge
Taylor & Francis Group

NEW YORK AND LONDON

First published in 2005 by Prufrock.Press Inc.

Published in 2021 by Routledge
605 Third Avenue, New York, NY 10017
2 Park Square, Milton Park, Abingdon, Oxon OX14 4RN

*Routledge is an imprint of the Taylor & Francis Group, an informa business.*

ISBN: 9781593631437 (pbk)

DOI: 10.4324/9781003239109

Common Core State Standards Alignment Sheet
# Thinking Through Analogies

## All lessons in this book align to the following standards.

| Grade Level | Common Core State Standards in ELA-Literacy |
|---|---|
| Grade 4 | L.4.4 Determine or clarify the meaning of unknown and multiple-meaning words and phrases based on grade 4 reading and content, choosing flexibly from a range of strategies. |
| Grade 5 | L.5.5 Demonstrate understanding of figurative language, word relationships, and nuances in word meanings.<br>L.5.6 Acquire and use accurately grade-appropriate general academic and domain-specific words and phrases, including those that signal contrast, addition, and other logical relationships (e.g., however, although, nevertheless, similarly, moreover, in addition). |
| Grade 6 | L.6.5 Demonstrate understanding of figurative language, word relationships, and nuances in word meanings.<br>L.6.6 Acquire and use accurately grade-appropriate general academic and domain-specific words and phrases; gather vocabulary knowledge when considering a word or phrase important to comprehension or expression. |
| Grade 7 | L.7.5 Demonstrate understanding of figurative language, word relationships, and nuances in word meanings.<br>L.7.6 Acquire and use accurately grade-appropriate general academic and domain-specific words and phrases; gather vocabulary knowledge when considering a word or phrase important to comprehension or expression. |

# Introduction

An analogy is a comparison between two things. It points out the similarities or likenesses between things that might be different in all other circumstances or respects. Analogies form the basis of much of our humor, poetry and metaphors. They draw a parallel between the common characteristics of two things, and they cause us to think analytically about forms, useages, structures and relationships. **Thinking Through Analogies** introduces students to several different types of analogies. By careful instruction, example and practice, students will gain the ability to recognize and solve all of these types of analogies.

**Thinking Through Analogies** teaches students to solve analogies by analyzing the elements of the puzzle and questioning the relationships that are presented. In this way, students become expert in **analyzing the relationship** between two things and mentally computing a similar relationship between two new things. Additionally, students will be exercising **flexible thinking** as they look for new relationships, creative combinations or untried similarities. These analogies will also build **vocabulary skills**. In many cases students will need to look up the meanings of words in order to establish the correct relationship.

Although there are a great variety of analogies, **Thinking Through Analogies** presents the most common types. By working through these exercises, students will build a repertoire of analogy types and they will sharpen their ability to discover how two things are related. Some of the types of analogies presented in this book are synonyms, antonyms, members of a hierarchy, and tools and their uses, to name only a few. After being introduced to each specific type of analogy, students are given many opportunities to apply their skills at solving the analogy, identifying the analogy when they are given examples, and also writing their own analogies.

It should be emphasized that although the analogies in this book are carefully thought out along the lines of well-defined categories of analogies, young minds sometimes find relationships that are not as obvious but in their own right merit consideration and praise. When students offer answers that are different from those that are indicated on the answer page, discuss their answers. You may find that they have developed a valid, logical line of reasoning. It is good, of course, to point out the more common train of thought. But some of our best analogies throughout history seem to compare things without any obvious relationship. Thus it is good to keep an open mind and maintain a degree of flexibility that unfortunately is missing in most tests and other instruments for measuring students' skills in thinking through analogies.

# Table of Contents

**Introducing:** **1. Synonyms**

example - yell is to shout as twelve is to dozen

or

yell : shout :: twelve : dozen

**2. Antonyms**

example - wealth is to poverty as dense is to sparse

or

wealth : poverty :: dense : sparse

---

**1. catch : capture :: docile : _____**
a. mean
b. wild
c. obedient
d. ugly

**2. system : method :: faith : _____**
a. trust
b. mistrust
c. manner
d. courtesy

**3. sympathy : pity ::**
**awkward : _____**
a. mourn
b. die
c. clumsy
d. puppy

**4. yell : whisper :: tame : _____**
a. docile
b. wild
c. animal
d. scream

**5. + : − :: × : _____**
a. #
b. %
c. ÷
d. ?

**6. empty : full :: awkward : _____**
a. graceful
b. clumsy
c. helpful
d. hollow

**7. main : primary :: labor : _____**
a. play
b. first
c. hard
d. work

**8. delay : stall :: allow : _____**
a. restrict
b. strict
c. late
d. permit

**9. prey : quarry :: strike : _____**
a. animal
b. hunt
c. hit
d. stripe

**10. first : last :: most : _____**
a. least
b. more
c. biggest
d. late

**11. polite : courteous ::**
**style : _____**
a. nice
b. pretty
c. ugly
d. fashion

**12. marsh : swamp ::**
**postpone : _____**
a. bog
b. prone
c. delay
d. cancel

**13. narrow : thin :: boulder : _____**
a. big
b. hard
c. shoulder
d. rock

**14. cheap : expensive ::**
**high : _____**
a. tall
b. building
c. costly
d. low

**Introducing:** 1. **Whole : part**
example - violin : string :: apple : core
2. **Part : whole**
example - string : violin :: core : apple
3. **General : specific**
example - noble : baron :: royalty : king
4. **Specific : general**
example - baron : noble :: king : royalty

1. car : tire :: tree : _____
   a. rubber
   b. limb
   c. wheel
   d. grow

2. book : chapter :: tractor : _____
   a. plowed
   b. read
   c. track
   d. motor

3. pie : dessert :: maple : _____
   a. tree
   b. eat
   c. sweet
   d. cut

4. bird : meadowlark ::
   flower : _____
   a. smell
   b. bright
   c. sing
   d. poppy

5. state : Nevada ::
   evergreen : _____
   a. pine
   b. needles
   c. Christmas
   d. cougar

6. plant : dandelion :: city : _____
   a. town
   b. country
   c. state
   d. Chicago

7. bicycle : pedal :: fireplace : _____
   a. burn
   b. mantel
   c. ride
   d. warm

8. piano : key :: typewriter : _____
   a. ribbon
   b. music
   c. write
   d. electric

9. foot : toe :: face : _____
   a. finger
   b. toenail
   c. nose
   d. arm

10. minuet : dance :: fox : _____
    a. trot
    b. fur
    c. animal
    d. trap

11. fish : trout :: insect : _____
    a. fox
    b. buzz
    c. katydid
    d. crawl

12. 1000 : number :: football : _____
    a. kick
    b. sport
    c. player
    d. 2000

13. roof : house :: wall : _____
    a. room
    b. straight
    c. square
    d. cracked

14. petal : flower :: eye : _____
    a. cry
    b. see
    c. blink
    d. potato

Introducing: 1. **Thing : characteristic**
example - star : shiny :: windmill : tall
2. **Characteristic : thing**
example - shiny : star :: tall : windmill
3. **Group : members**
example - herd : cow :: flock : sheep
4. **Members : group**
example - cow : herd :: sheep : flock

---

1. **ant : tiny :: rabbit : _____**
   a. foot
   b. carrots
   c. soft
   d. scratch

2. **swift : deer :: slow : _____**
   a. turtle
   b. sluggish
   c. fast
   d. crawl

3. **partridge : covey :: card : _____**
   a. play
   b. square
   c. spade
   d. deck

4. **pair : sock :: grove : _____**
   a. glove
   b. grow
   c. green
   d. tree

5. **school : fish :: pack : _____**
   a. student
   b. wolf
   c. bite
   d. swim

6. **fire : hot :: candy : _____**
   a. lick
   b. mouth
   c. sweet
   d. cold

7. **sharp : sword :: smooth : _____**
   a. cut
   b. rough
   c. clear
   d. glass

8. **jury : juror :: swarm : _____**
   a. warm
   b. swim
   c. bee
   d. sting

9. **flock : chicken :: squadron : _____**
   a. airplane
   b. air
   c. crash
   d. cluck

10. **team : player :: class : _____**
    a. desk
    b. paper
    c. student
    d. door

11. **roses : bouquet :: ponies : _____**
    a. hoof
    b. mane
    c. herd
    d. little

12. **caravan : truck :: gang : _____**
    a. drive
    b. fight
    c. sing
    d. outlaw

13. **ice : cold :: pickle : _____**
    a. eat
    b. barrel
    c. sour
    d. hamburger

14. **lemonade : cool :: rock : _____**
    a. hard
    b. baby
    c. roll
    d. drink

**Introducing: 1. Thing or place : what it might contain or house**
example - fort : soldier :: court : judge

**2. Contents : place or thing containing it.**
example - soldier : fort :: judge : court

---

1. vineyard : grape vines ::
   orchard : _____
   a. roses
   b. fruit trees
   c. cattle
   d. strawberries

2. hive : bee :: library : _____
   a. candy bar
   b. socks
   c. book
   d. pencil

3. nest : bird :: burrow : _____
   a. owl
   b. kitten
   c. banana
   d. woodchuck

4. papers : desk :: food : _____
   a. refrigerator
   b. closet
   c. berry
   d. lettuce

5. fire : fireplace :: car : _____
   a. tire
   b. mechanic
   c. garage
   d. wreck

6. barracks : soldiers ::
   anthill : _____
   a. robins
   b. ants
   c. mountains
   d. anteaters

7. ship : sailor :: nest : _____
   a. cowboy
   b. bluebird
   c. Indian
   d. buffalo

8. fish : aquarium :: plant : _____
   a. green
   b. grow
   c. terrarium
   d. lettuce

9. bee : apiary :: bird : _____
   a. sky
   b. wing
   c. aviary
   d. beak

10. jail : prisoner :: hospital : _____
    a. owl
    b. patients
    c. door
    d. clock

11. flour : pantry :: milk : _____
    a. refrigerator
    b. chocolate
    c. water
    d. spoiled

12. closet : clothes ::
    breadbox : _____
    a. house
    b. money
    c. bread
    d. matches

13. garden : cucumber ::
    crib : _____
    a. tomatoes
    b. dog
    c. baby
    d. stroller

14. flower : vase :: water : _____
    a. milk
    b. lake
    c. car
    d. bag

In this lesson no new types of analogies will be introduced. Instead we will review analogies that you already know how to solve. It is very important to think about the relationship between the first two words before trying to choose the word that completes the second pair of words.

1. **pardon : forgive ::**
   **scarce : _____**
   a. plentiful
   b. scarey
   c. rare
   d. common

2. **heavy : light :: scarce : _____**
   a. plentiful
   b. dull
   c. rare
   d. difficult

3. **day : hour :: week : _____**
   a. minute
   b. second
   c. month
   d. day

4. **fairy tale : Snow White ::**
   **sandwich : _____**
   a. delicious
   b. hamburger
   c. bread
   d. milk

5. **pride : lion :: band : _____**
   a. musician
   b. music
   c. rubber
   d. brave

6. **elephant : wrinkled ::**
   **chalk : _____**
   a. write
   b. skin
   c. blackboard
   d. white

7. **volcano : lava :: geyser : _____**
   a. steam
   b. Old Faithful
   c. mountain
   d. magma

8. **observe : watch :: grieve : _____**
   a. peer
   b. see
   c. mourn
   d. funeral

9. **certain : sure :: trip : _____**
   a. naturally
   b. graceful
   c. journey
   d. daily

10. **aid : help :: kind : _____**
    a. cruel
    b. brisk
    c. coward
    d. merciful

11. **urban : rural :: courage : _____**
    a. bravery
    b. lion
    c. suburban
    d. cowardice

12. **nourish : starve ::**
    **rudeness : _____**
    a. courtesy
    b. hunger
    c. discourtesy
    d. feed

13. **month : week :: year : _____**
    a. time
    b. month
    c. decade
    d. century

14. **toffee : candy ::**
    **greyhound : _____**
    a. fast
    b. fleet
    c. dog
    d. rapid

Directions: Identify each analogy as to its correct type. Choose only one answer.

**1. peaceful : tranquil**
a. synonyms
b. antonyms
c. whole : part
d. part : whole
e. general : specific
f. specific : general

**2. forward : backward**
a. synonyms
b. antonyms
c. whole : part
d. part : whole
e. general : specific
f. specific : general

**3. corn : stalk**
a. whole : part
b. part : whole
c. general : specific
d. antonyms
e. thing : characteristic
f. characteristic : thing

**4. color: green**
a. whole : part
b. part : whole
c. general : specific
d. specific : general
e. thing : characteristic
f. antonyms

**5. squad : soldier**
a. synonyms
b. group : member
c. member : group
d. antonyms
e. general : specific
f. specific : general

**6. ball : round**
a. thing : characteristic
b. characteristic : thing
c. group : member
d. member : group
e. whole : part
f. antonyms

**7. holster : gun**
a. antonyms
b. member : group
c. group : member
d. general : specific
e. container : contents
f. contents : container

**8. door : squeaky**
a. synonyms
b. antonyms
c. group : member
d. container : contents
e. thing : characteristic
f. characteristic : thing

**9. cluster : grapes**
a. antonyms
b. thing : characteristic
c. group : member
d. member : group
e. general : specific
f. specific : general

**10. fruit : apple**
a. synonyms
b. antonyms
c. whole : part
d. general : specific
e. thing : characteristic
f. member : group

**11. north : south**
a. synonyms
b. antonyms
c. whole : part
d. general : specific
e. thing : characteristic
f. member : group

**12. shrewd : clever**
a. synonyms
b. antonyms
c. whole : part
d. general : specific
e. thing : characteristic
f. member : group

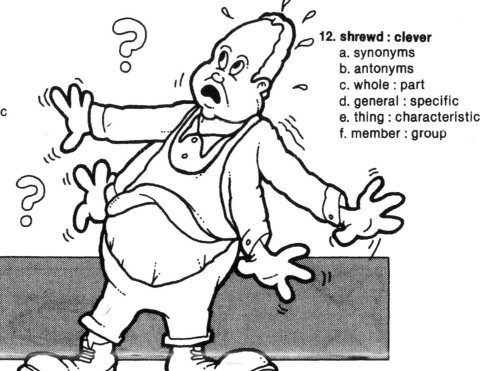

This is your chance to write your own analogies. Look at the first two words that are given and think about the relationship between them. Then find two other words with the same relationship that will complete the sentence. Be original and creative!

1. Sad : happy :: _____ : _____

2. notable : insignificant :: _____ : _____

3. punctual : tardy :: _____ : _____

4. flower : fragrant :: _____ : _____

5. masculine : feminine :: _____ : _____

6. chocolate milk : drink :: _____ : _____

7. pages : book :: _____ : _____

8. fire : hot :: _____ : _____

9. animal : horse :: _____ : _____

10. school : fish :: _____ : _____

11. Joyce : name :: _____ : _____

12. summer : winter :: _____ : _____

13. tribe : Indians :: _____ : _____

14. granite : rock :: _____ : _____

15. fish : trout :: _____ : _____

16. smooth : velvet :: _____ : _____

17. _____ : _____ :: _____ : _____

18. _____ : _____ :: _____ : _____

**Introducing:** 1. **Worker : tool they might use**
example - carpenter : saw :: programmer : computer
2. **Tool : worker**
example - saw : carpenter :: computer : programmer
3. **Two members of the same class**
example - waltz : polka :: potato : turnip

---

**1. nurse : thermometer ::**
**doctor : \_\_\_\_**
a. wound
b. scapel
c. uniform
d. injury

**2. wrench : mechanic ::**
**brush : \_\_\_\_**
a. car
b. paint
c. painter
d. splash

**3. salamander : frog ::**
**trumpet : \_\_\_\_\_**
a. croak
b. music
c. brass
d. cornet

**4. baseball : hockey ::**
**ice cream : \_\_\_\_**
a. melt
b. vanilla
c. pudding
d. cone

**5. balls : juggler ::**
**ax : \_\_\_\_**
a. tree
b. lumberjack
c. chop
d. saw

**6. cowboy : lariat :: artist : \_\_\_\_**
a. art
b. bandana
c. landscape
d. easel

**7. CB radio : truck driver ::**
**baton : \_\_\_\_**
a. conductor
b. stick
c. music
d. wheel

**8. soda : milk ::**
**veterinarian : \_\_\_\_\_**
a. dog
b. dentist
c. animal
d. medicine

**9. cashew : peanut ::**
**blouse : \_\_\_\_**
a. peanut butter
b. button
c. shirt
d. silk

**10. farmer : tractor ::**
**engineer : \_\_\_\_**
a. bridge
b. gun
c. calculator
d. dog

**11. microphone : singer ::**
**blow dryer : \_\_\_\_**
a. beautician
b. hair
c. hot
d. curls

**12. teacher : chalk ::**
**draftsman : \_\_\_\_**
a. draft
b. drafting board
c. tree
d. horn

**13. blonde : brunette ::**
**sedan : \_\_\_\_\_**
a. brown
b. wheel
c. convertible
d. drive

**14. needle : seamstress ::**
**telephone : \_\_\_\_**
a. ring
b. dial
c. cord
d. salesman

**Introducing:** 1. **Thing : something it does**
example - duck : migrate :: groundhog : hibernate
2. **Something it does : thing**
example - migrate : duck :: hibernate : groundhog
3. **Thing : product**
example - cow : milk :: tree : lumber
4. **Product : thing**
example - milk : cow :: lumber : tree
5. **Singular : plural**
example - child : children :: man : men
6. **Plural : singular**
example - children : child :: men : man

---

**1. burn : fire :: cut : _____**
a. sore
b. finger
c. knife
d. sharp

**2. wool : sheep :: egg : _____**
a. fried
b. hen
c. bacon
d. candy

**3. pin : pins :: egg : _____**
a. hen
b. candy
c. eggs
d. basket

**4. bell : ring :: horn : _____**
a. goat
b. toot
c. copper
d. plenty

**5. man : run :: horse : _____**
a. hoof
b. shoe
c. boy
d. gallop

**6. bee : honey :: farmer : _____**
a. plow
b. crop
c. harrow
d. rainfall

**7. oil : sunflower :: flour : _____**
a. wheat
b. chicken
c. bread
d. white

**8. knives : knife :: sheep : _____**
a. lamb
b. sheep
c. goat
d. wool

**9. shoe : shoes :: ox : _____**
a. wagon
b. big
c. strong
d. oxen

**10. pig : bacon :: cotton : _____**
a. cloth
b. soft
c. white
d. grow

**11. fruit : orchard :: grape : _____**
a. purple
b. wine
c. vineyard
d. juice

**12. bee : buzz :: bird : _____**
a. worm
b. nest
c. robin
d. chirp

**13. tick : clock :: ring : _____**
a. round
b. bell
c. gold
d. beep

**14. rooster : crow :: kitten : _____**
a. soft
b. fur
c. striped
d. meow

**Introducing:**
**1. Parts of a hierarchy**
example - private : sergeant :: freshman : senior
**2. Instrument for measuring : what is being measured**
example - barometer : atmospheric pressure :: clock : time
**3. What is being measured : Instrument for measuring**
example - atmospheric pressure : barometer :: time : clock

---

**1. serf : lord :: noble : _____**
a. peasant
b. king
c. manor
d. castle

**2. nickel : dime :: dime : _____**
a. money
b. coin
c. quarter
d. silver

**3. drone : queen :: player : _____**
a. coach
b. sport
c. athlete
d. uniform

**4. cub scout : boy scout ::
boy scout : _____**
a. cub scout
b. eagle scout
c. merit badge
d. camping

**5. boss : worker :: captain : _____**
a. ship
b. sea
c. anchor
d. sailor

**6. captain : admiral ::
mayor : _____**
a. city
b. county
c. governor
d. state

**7. anemometer : wind velocity ::
hour glass : _____**
a. sand
b. time
c. rain
d. speed

**8. temperature : thermometer ::
time : _____**
a. calendar
b. odometer
c. speedometer
d. day

**9. ruler : distance ::
sphygmomanometer : _____**
a. light
b. speed
c. blood pressure
d. distance

**10. town : county :: state : _____**
a. Illinois
b. nation
c. county
d. township

**11. pint : quart :: quart : _____**
a. ice cream
b. pint
c. gallon
d. liquid

**12. disciple : leader ::
warrior : _____**
a. chief
b. spear
c. feather
d. weapon

**13. senator : president ::
reporter : _____**
a. congress
b. editor
c. article
d. newspaper

**14. scale : weight :: ruler : _____**
a. distance
b. volume
c. time
d. weight

**Introducing:**

1. **Similar things of different degrees - less : more or more : less**
   example - cool : frigid :: warm : hot
   example - frigid : cool :: hot : warm
2. **Device : what is required to make it work**
   example - camera : film :: phonograph : record
3. **Spatial relationships**
   example - doughnut : hole :: moat : castle

---

**1. hill : mountain :: brook : _____**
   a. cave
   b. river
   c. ocean
   d. mound

**2. computer : software :: car : _____**
   a. gasoline
   b. typewriter
   c. gymnast
   d. insect

**3. tapestry : wall :: carpet : _____**
   a. ceiling
   b. floor
   c. vacuum cleaner
   d. weave

**4. grove : forest :: pond : _____**
   a. tree
   b. water
   c. lake
   d. tadpole

**5. ditch : ravine :: crack : _____**
   a. cricket
   b. crevice
   c. break
   d. cracker

**6. spool : thread :: reel : _____**
   a. fishing line
   b. kite
   c. rod
   d. steel

**7. pen : ink :: gun _____**
   a. trigger
   b. bullet
   c. holster
   d. rifle

**8. fear : phobia :: upset : _____**
   a. hysterical
   b. happiest
   c. calm
   d. lazy

**9. balloon : string :: ship :: _____**
   a. sail
   b. hull
   c. anchor
   d. passenger

**10. frame : picture :: fence _____**
   a. yard
   b. photograph
   c. bed
   d. wooden

**11. pale : livid :: firm : _____**
   a. soft
   b. white
   c. dull
   d. rigid

**12. small : minute :: large : _____**
   a. big
   b. tiny
   c. gigantic
   d. rough

**13. button : shirt :: lash : _____**
   a. door
   b. eyelid
   c. popcorn
   d. sweater

**14. moon : earth :: earth :: _____**
   a. planet
   b. moon
   c. sun
   d. atmosphere

In this lesson no new analogies will be introduced. Instead you will review types of analogies that you have already learned how to solve. It is very important to think of the relationship between the first two words before you try to select the word that completes the second pair of words.

1. **left : right :: up :** _____
   a. high
   b. down
   c. straight
   d. low

2. **pacific : peaceful :: poise :** _____
   a. grace
   b. awkwardness
   c. happiness
   d. revenge

3. **excuse : pardon :: clothing :** _____
   a. coat
   b. forgive
   c. garment
   d. socks

4. **decade : year :: century :** _____
   a. ten
   b. decade
   c. time
   d. past

5. **shape : triangular :: country :** _____
   a. big
   b. nation
   c. United States
   d. county

6. **fleet : taxicab :: bunch :** _____
   a. fast
   b. banana
   c. heavy
   d. eat

7. **road : bumpy :: paint :** _____
   a. painter
   b. wall
   c. house
   d. sticky

8. **rake : gardener :: pick :** _____
   a. barber
   b. tooth
   c. sharp
   d. miner

9. **hummingbird : cardinal :: monarch :** _____
   a. bird
   b. bee
   c. butterfly
   d. swallowtail

10. **top : spin :: ball :** _____
    a. round
    b. bounce
    c. air
    d. bat

11. **goat : angora :: elephant :** _____
    a. herd
    b. big
    c. wrinkled
    d. ivory

12. **foxes : fox :: leaves :** _____
    a. left
    b. goes
    c. leaf
    d. tree

13. **student : teacher :: teacher :** _____
    a. classroom
    b. chalk
    c. prinicpal
    d. apple

14. **seismograph : earthquake :: Geiger counter** _____
    a. radioactivity
    b. temperature
    c. air pressure
    d. distance

In this lesson no new types of analogies will be introduced. Instead you will review anaologies that you have already learned how to solve. It is very important that you think about the relationship between the first two words before trying to select the word that completes the second pair of words.

1. **pain : agony :: costly : _____**
   a. cheap
   b. exorbitant
   c. hurtful
   d. reasonable

2. **cold : hot :: light : _____**
   a. bright
   b. warm
   c. dark
   d. switch

3. **mourn : rejoice :: dawn : _____**
   a. dusk
   b. morning
   c. sun up
   d. day

4. **work : toil :: utterly : _____**
   a. speak
   b. thoroughly
   c. carefully
   d. small

5. **authentic : genuine :: menancing : _____**
   a. helping
   b. calling
   c. threatening
   d. beseeching

6. **mimic : imitate :: crestfallen : _____**
   a. act
   b. injured
   c. dead
   d. woebegone

7. **herd : cow :: flock : _____**
   a. fleece
   b. herd
   c. sheep
   d. nine

8. **isthmus : Panama :: mountain : _____**
   a. high
   b. hill
   c. rugged
   d. Pike's Peak

9. **snake : reptile :: democracy : _____**
   a. freedom
   b. monarchy
   c. government
   d. United States

10. **constellation : star :: committee : _____**
    a. people
    b. chairman
    c. talk
    d. conference

11. **lollipop : hard :: chocolate : _____**
    a. kiss
    b. candy
    c. cacao
    d. brown

12. **soothing : music :: fluffy : _____**
    a. soft
    b. cloud
    c. hard
    d. flat

13. **airplane : crop duster :: crop : _____**
    a. cotton
    b. cut
    c. short
    d. airplane

14. **maple : elm :: rose : _____**
    a. red
    b. fragrant
    c. peony
    d. bud

Directions: Identify each type of analogy. Choose only one answer.

**1. weighty : heavy**
 a. synonyms
 b. antonyms
 c. whole: part
 d. part : whole
 e. general : specific
 f. specific : general

**2. morning : evening**
 a. synomyns
 b. antonyms
 c. whole : part
 d. general : specific
 e. thing : characteristic
 f. member : group

**3. bird : wing**
 a. synonyms
 b. whole : part
 c. part : whole
 d. general : specific
 e. specific : general
 f. thing : characteristic

**4. river : Mississippi**
 a. synonyms
 b. whole : part
 c. part : whole
 d. general : specific
 e. specific : general
 f. thing : characteristic

**5. litter : kitten**
 a. thing : characteristic
 b. antonyms
 c. group : member
 d. member : group
 e. specific : general
 f. general : specific

**6. pill : bitter**
 a. thing : characteristic
 b. antonyms
 c. group: member
 d. synonyms
 e. specific : general
 f. general : specific

**7. holster : gun**
 a. synonyms
 b. antonyms
 c. container : contents
 d. general : specific
 e. specific : general
 f. thing : characteristic

**8. astronaut : space suit**
 a. general : specific
 b. specific : general
 c. worker : tool
 d. tool : worker
 e. members of the same class
 f. antonyms

**9. collie : cocker spaniel**
 a. general : specific
 b. specific : general
 c. worker : tool
 d. tool : worker
 e. members of the same class
 f. antonyms

**10. river : flow**
 a. general : specific
 b. specific : general
 c. worker : tool
 d. tool : worker
 e. thing : what it does
 f. thing : product

**11. sturgeon : caviar**
 a. general : specific
 b. specific : general
 c. worker : tool
 d. tool : worker
 e. thing : what it does
 f. thing : product

**12. woman : women**
 a. thing : what it does
 b. thing : product
 c. singular : plural
 d. plural : singular
 e. product : source
 f. general : specific

This is your chance to write your own analogies. Look at the first two words that are given and think about the relationship between them. Then find two other words with the same relationship that will complete the sentence. Be original and creative!

1. cold : ice :: _____ : _____

2. troop : soldiers :: _____ : _____

3. elephants : herd :: _____ : _____

4. patch : strawberries :: _____ : _____

5. flowers : bouquet :: _____ : _____

6. yes : no :: _____ : _____

7. Catholic : religion :: _____ : _____

8. cheat : defraud :: _____ : _____

9. cherry : fruit :: _____ : _____

10. game : chess :: _____ : _____

11. shoe : foot :: _____ : _____

12. frame : picture :: _____ : _____

13. words : dictionary :: _____ : _____

14. seldom : often :: _____ : _____

15. Ford : car :: _____ : _____

16. vein : blood :: _____ : _____

17. _____ : _____ :: _____ : _____

18. _____ : _____ :: _____ : _____

Introducing: 1. **Things that go together**
example - bread : butter :: knife : fork
2. **Regional synonyms**
example - green beans : string beans :: cantaloupe : muskmelon
3. **Things : foundations or**
**Foundations : things**
example - House : basement :: tree : root

---

**1. person : feet :: pyramid : _____**
a. point
b. three
c. base
d. Egypt

**2. skunk : polecat ::**
**groundhog : _____**
a. smell
b. woodchuck
c. fur
d. burrow

**3. fish : chips :: shoe : _____**
a. sole
b. string
c. heel
d. sock

**4. roasting ear : corn on the cob ::**
**husk : _____**
a. root
b. kernel
c. shuck
d. leave

**5. rocking chair : rocker ::**
**roller skate : _____**
a. roller
b. rink
c. key
d. fall

**6. bagel : lox :: horse : _____**
a. lion
b. carriage
c. butterfly
d. cheese

**7. hot cakes : pancakes ::**
**soda : _____**
a. glass
b. ice
c. pop
d. sugar

**8. table : legs :: wagon : _____**
a. wheels
b. seat
c. shelf
d. canvas

**9. salt : pepper :: cup : _____**
a. table
b. crack
c. saucer
d. spoon

**10. bride : groom :: pen : _____**
a. pin
b. ink
c. pan
d. stone

**11. tooth : root :: statue : _____**
a. marble
b. pedestal
c. sculptor
d. painting

**12. champagne : caviar ::**
**cheese : _____**
a. Swiss
b. moldy
c. stale
d. crackers

**13. thunder : lightning ::**
**ghost : _____**
a. goblin
b. rain
c. spooky
d. strained

**14. mattress : bed springs ::**
**ocean : _____**
a. water
b. salty
c. fish
d. ocean floor

**Introducing:**
1. **Thing : function**
   example - spoon : stir :: razor : shave
2. **Function : thing**
   example - stir : spoon :: shave : razor
3. **Male : female**
   example - rooster : hen :: bull : cow
4. **Female : male**
   example - hen : rooster :: cow : bull
5. **Adult : offspring**
   example - pig : piglet :: goose : gosling
6. **Offspring : adult**
   example - piglet : pig :: gosling : goose

---

**1. pen : write :: calculator : _____**
a. numbers
b. compute
c. paper
d. display

**2. cook : stove :: cut : _____**
a. paper
b. finger
c. bandage
d. knife

**3. ram : ewe :: steward : _____**
a. stewardess
b. train
c. airplane
d. captain

**4. actor : actress :: gander : _____**
a. stare
b. awkward
c. goose
d. feathers

**5. chicken : chick :: duck : _____**
a. drake
b. swim
c. webbed
d. duckling

**6. puppy : dog :: kitten : _____**
a. meow
b. fur
c. soft
d. cat

**7. crayon : color :: candle : _____**
a. light
b. wax
c. candle holder
d. drip

**8. cut : saw :: sew : _____**
a. dress
b. stick
c. needle
d. seam

**9. drake : duck :: buck : _____**
a. skin
b. dollar
c. doe
d. brake

**10. woman : man :: girl : _____**
a. mother
b. dress
c. female
d. boy

**11. horse : colt :: wolf : _____**
a. lamb
b. gray
c. Red Riding Hood
d. cub

**12. calf : cow :: lamb : _____**
a. fleecy
b. spring
c. Little Bo Peep
d. sheep

**13. brush : paint :: ball : _____**
a. round
b. bounce
c. inflated
d. bat

**14. waiter : waitress : father ::**
_____
a. order
b. man
c. mother
d. children

**Introducing:** 1. **Thing : outer covering**
example - cake : icing :: racoon : fur
2. **Outer covering : thing**
example - icing : cake :: fur : racoon
3. **Thing : top**
example - house : roof :: man : hat
4. **Top : thing**
example - roof : house :: man : hat

---

1. **fish : scales :: person :** _____
   a. gills
   b. walk
   c. swim
   d. skin

2. **peel : banana :: feathers :** _____
   a. pillow
   b. fluffy
   c. bird
   d. soft

3. **woman : bonnet :: king :** _____
   a. crown
   b. jewels
   c. gold
   d. royalty

4. **peak : mountain :: hair :** _____
   a. snarl
   b. comb
   c. head
   d. snow

5. **duckling : down ::**
   **peanut :** _____
   a. bread
   b. brown
   c. salty
   d. shell

6. **bark : tree :: enamel :** _____
   a. bush
   b. tooth
   c. rabbit
   d. fur

7. **turtle : shell :: apple :** _____
   a. tree
   b. red
   c. teacher
   d. skin

8. **bread : crust :: corn :** _____
   a. meal
   b. bread
   c. pop
   d. husk

9. **feather : turkey :: shell :** _____
   a. crack
   b. lobster
   c. hen
   d. sea

10. **crust : pie :: atmosphere :** _____
    a. air
    b. stratosphere
    c. earth
    d. polluted

11. **lid : kettle :: summit :** _____
    a. top
    b. base
    c. hill
    d. skillet

12. **rooster : comb :: chief :** _____
    a. warrior
    b. tent
    c. leader
    d. head dress

13. **cardinal : crest ::**
    **antelope :** _____
    a. deer
    b. doe
    c. antlers
    d. skin

14. **surface : ocean ::**
    **penthouse :** _____
    a. skyscraper
    b. ship
    c. elevator
    d. expensive

**Introducing:**
**1. Worker : product**
example - miner : coal :: sawyer : lumber
**2. Product : worker**
example - coal : miner :: lumber : sawyer
**3. Symbol : thing represented**
example - olive branch : peace :: owl :: wisdom
**4. Thing represented : symbol**
example - peace : olive branch :: wisdom : owl
**5. Worker : job location**
example - logger : forest :: fisherman : ocean
**6. Job location : worker**
example - forest : logger :: ocean :: fisherman

---

**1. baker : bread :: sculptor : _____**
   a. chisel
   b. statue
   c. aroma
   d. hammer

**2. soybeans : farmer ::**
   **salmon : _____**
   a. fisherman
   b. net
   c. river
   d. fish

**3. scales : justice ::**
   **laurel wreath : _____**
   a. tree
   b. Roman
   c. accomplishment
   d. head

**4. peace : dove ::**
   **good luck : _____**
   a. lucky
   b. bad luck
   c. happenstance
   d. horse shoe

**5. farmer : field :: miner : _____**
   a. coal
   b. pick
   c. mine
   d. lamp

**6. office : secretary ::**
   **school : _____**
   a. bell
   b. desk
   c. year
   d. teacher

**7. seamstress : dress ::**
   **author : _____**
   a. typewriter
   b. writer
   c. book
   d. Mark Twain

**8. suit : tailor :: shoe : _____**
   a. leather
   b. lace
   c. cobbler
   d. store

**9. four leaf clover : good luck ::**
   **white : _____**
   a. black
   b. purity
   c. calendar
   d. statue

**10. royalty : fleur-de-lis ::**
   **plenty : _____**
   a. cornucopia
   b. famine
   c. drought
   d. roses

**11. doctor : hospital ::**
   **librarian : _____**
   a. book
   b. quiet
   c. drug store
   d. library

**12. court room : judge ::**
   **church : _____**
   a. pew
   b. steeple
   c. hymn
   d. minister

**13. printer : newspaper ::**
   **photographer : _____**
   a. film
   b. darkroom
   c. photograph
   d. baby

**14. bee : honey :: beaver : _____**
   a. castor
   b. birch
   c. dam
   d. kit

**Introducing:** 1. **Container : what is contained**
example - balloon : air :: canteen : water
**What is contained : container**
example - air : balloon :: water : canteen
2. **Things that stick together**
example - barnacle : ship :: stamp : envelope
3. **Person : area of interest**
example - astronomer : stars :: paleontologist : fossils
**Area of interest : person**
example - stars : astronomer :: fossils : paleontologist
4. **Thing : what it might become**
example - coal : diamond :: peat : coal
**What it might become : thing**
example - diamond : coal :: coal : peat

1. **pillow : feathers ::**
**flower pot : _____**
a. terra cotta
b. soil
c. cracked
d. red

2. **soup : bowl :: oil : _____**
a. float
b. crude
c. refinery
d. barrel

3. **fly : flypaper :: lint : _____**
a. fuzzy
b. speck
c. sweater
d. brush

4. **dog : cockleburr :: fish : _____**
a. water
b. swim
c. perch
d. leech

5. **philatelist : stamp ::**
**numismatist : _____**
a. news
b. group
c. envelope
d. coin

6. **shorthand : stenographer ::**
**maps : _____**
a. secretary
b. cartographer
c. topography
d. population

7. **nectar : honey :: cream : _____**
a. cow
b. spoiled
c. sweet
d. butter

8. **pickle : cucumber ::**
**sauerkraut : _____**
a. sour
b. hot dog
c. cabbage
d. mustard

9. **canister : flour ::**
**sandbag : _____**
a. flood
b. sand
c. river
d. burlap

10. **iron : magnet :: stamp : _____**
a. lick
b. letter
c. envelope
d. metal

11. **mind : psychologist ::**
**body : _____**
a. exercise
b. food
c. injury
d. physician

12. **tadpole : frog :: acorn : _____**
a. pecan
b. squirrel
c. autumn
d. oak

13. **psychologist : behavior ::**
**numismatist : _____**
a. numbers
b. coins
c. collector
d. numerous

14. **cacao : chocolate ::**
**intern : _____**
a. candy
b. hospital
c. study
d. doctor

In this lesson you will not learn about any new types of analogies. Instead you will have a chance to review several types of analogies that you have already learned how to solve. It is very important for you to think about the relationship between the first two words before trying to select the word that completes the second pair of words.

**1. reasonable : sensible ::**
   **annoyed : _____**
   a. happy
   b. pleased
   c. irritated
   d. logical

**2. night : day :: summer : _____**
   a. winter
   b. spring
   c. hot
   d. season

**3. church : steeple :: poem : _____**
   a. Longfellow
   b. poet
   c. stanza
   d. recite

**4. hat : sombrero ::**
   **nursery rhyme : _____**
   a. Little Bo Peep
   b. child
   c. read
   d. nurse

**5. bevy : quail :: gaggle : _____**
   a. fish
   b. fly
   c. swim
   d. geese

**6. fuse : short :: whale : _____**
   a. mammal
   b. huge
   c. swim
   d. spume

**7. lock : key :: quiver : _____**
   a. tremble
   b. arrow
   c. archer
   d. bow

**8. scissors : barber :: net : _____**
   a. fisherman
   b. fish
   c. string
   d. butterfly

**9. apple : pear :: beef : _____**
   a. meat
   b. pork
   c. cow
   d. cook

**10. turtle : crawl :: snake : _____**
   a. skin
   b. slither
   c. rattler
   d. fang

**11. rose : attar :: oyster : _____**
   a. ocean
   b. fry
   c. lobster
   d. pearl

**12. baby : babies :: cookie : _____**
   a. jar
   b. chocolate chip
   c. milk
   d. cookies

**13. cardinal : pope ::**
   **fireman : _____**
   a. fire
   b. hose
   c. chief
   d. truck

**14. peanut butter : jelly ::**
   **Romeo : _____**
   a. hero
   b. Juliet
   c. balcony
   d. play

In this lesson no new types of analogies will be introduced. Instead you will review analogies that you have already learned how to solve. It is very important that you think about the relationship between the first two words before trying to select the word that completes the second pair of words.

1. **dog : cat :: spaghetti : _____**
   a. food
   b. Italian
   c. meatball
   d. eat

2. **car : road :: train : _____**
   a. tracks
   b. engineer
   c. fireman
   d. coal

3. **prism : refract :: hose : _____**
   a. water pressure
   b. garden
   c. stocking
   d. spray

4. **cantaloupe : rind :: kitten : _____**
   a. cat
   b. pet
   c. fur
   d. claw

5. **cabinet : carpenter :: blanket : _____**
   a. bed
   b. warm
   c. striped
   d. weaver

6. **skull and crossbones : death :: rabbit's foot : _____**
   a. bunny
   b. good luck
   c. carrots
   d. hutch

7. **stage : singer :: supermarket : _____**
   a. groceries
   b. checker
   c. bargain
   d. line

8. **trash can : trash :: piggy bank : _____**
   a. glass
   b. child
   c. pennies
   d. rob

9. **paint : wall :: icing : _____**
   a. ceiling
   b. frosting
   c. vanilla
   d. cake

10. **geologist : minerals :: agronomist : _____**
    a. money
    b. farming
    c. ancient
    d. tracks

11. **cider : vinegar :: milk : _____**
    a. cow
    b. cartoon
    c. cheese
    d. calcium

12. **aggravate : vex :: muggy : _____**
    a. mug
    b. arid
    c. humid
    d. cold

13. **peaceful : quarrelsome :: dull : _____**
    a. knife
    b. light
    c. sharp
    d. dulls

14. **glasses : lens :: coat : _____**
    a. wool
    b. warm
    c. fur
    d. cuff

**25**   © 2005 Taylor & Francis - Thinking Through Analogies

In this lesson no new types of analogies will be introduced. Instead you will review analogies that you have already learned how to solve. It is very important that you think about the relationship between the first two words before trying to select the word that completes the second pair of words.

1. **wheel : spoke :: chair : _____**
   a. round
   b. sit
   c. leg
   d. tire

2. **grain : corn :: gem : _____**
   a. gym
   b. gems
   c. diamond
   d. polish

3. **clump : trees : school : _____**
   a. leaves
   b. fish
   c. education
   d. grass

4. **mirror : reflective :: adjective : _____**
   a. descriptive
   b. speech
   c. adverb
   d. light

5. **comb : honey :: lake : _____**
   a. shore
   b. polluted
   c. boat
   d. water

6. **hunter : gun :: sailor : _____**
   a. seasick
   b. captain
   c. rope
   d. navy

7. **oils : watercolors :: granite : _____**
   a. rock
   b. limestone
   c. hard
   d. sculpt

8. **prism : refract :: mirror : _____**
   a. looking glass
   b. cracked
   c. reflect
   d. shiny

9. **sheep : wool :: flax : _____**
   a. yellow
   b. ripe
   c. linen
   d. perfume

10. **tooth : teeth :: mouse : _____**
    a. rodent
    b. cheese
    c. trap
    d. mice

11. **student : teacher :: mailman : _____**
    a. mail
    b. postage
    c. stamp
    d. postmaster

12. **speedometer : speed :: protractor : _____**
    a. compass
    b. math
    c. angles
    d. circle

13. **French fries : hamburger :: shoes : _____**
    a. leather
    b. socks
    c. running
    d. sandles

14. **stop sign : post :: flag : _____**
    a. nation
    b. unfurl
    c. pole
    d. salute

This is your chance to write your own analogies. Look at the first two words and think about the relationship between them. Then find two other words with the same relationship that will complete the sentence. Be original and creative!

1. photographer : camera :: _____ : _____

2. pear : apple :: _____ : _____

3. instrument : musician :: _____ : _____

4. dog : bark :: _____ : _____

5. domino : dominoes :: _____ : _____

6. sheep : wool :: _____ : _____

7. January : October ::: _____ : _____

8. energy : sun :: _____ : _____

9. tachometer : velocity :: _____ : _____

10. first : second :: _____ : _____

11. run : gallop :: _____ : _____

12. noon : lunch :: _____ : _____

13. bridge : water :: _____ : _____

14. earth : solar system :: _____ : _____

15. tired : exhausted :: _____ : _____

16. add : subtract :: _____ : _____

17. _____ : _____ :: _____ : _____

18. _____ : _____ :: _____ : _____

In this lesson no new types of analogies will be introduced. Instead you will review analogies that you have already learned how to solve. Remember to study the relationship between the first two words before trying to select the word that completes the second pair of words.

1. **abrupt : sudden :: house :** _____
   a. build
   b. carpenter
   c. dwelling
   d. brick

2. **advocate : recommend :: provoke :** _____
   a. irritate
   b. help
   c. happy
   d. joke

3. **future : past :: dead :** _____
   a. animal
   b. kill
   c. alive
   d. deceased

4. **birth : death :: simple :** _____
   a. easy
   b. foolish
   c. sample
   d. complex

5. **ship : mast :: airplane :** _____
   a. landing
   b. ailerons
   c. pilot
   d. air

6. **clock : hand :: peach :** _____
   a. apple
   b. orchard
   c. pit
   d. sherbert

7. **collar : blouse :: dial :** _____
   a. telephone
   b. shirt
   c. turn
   d. ring

8. **book : dictionary :: ruler :** _____
   a. encyclopedia
   b. emperor
   c. yard
   d. throne

9. **Niagara : waterfall :: clarinet :** _____
   a. flute
   b. music
   c. instrument
   d. river

10. **motorcade : car :: sheaf :** _____
    a. truck
    b. highway
    c. drive
    d. stalk

11. **fireman : battalion :: musicians :** _____
    a. fire
    b. instruments
    c. music
    d. band

12. **paper : torn :: ice cream :** _____
    a. melting
    b. eat
    c. cone
    d. lick

13. **rusty : metal :: rotten :** _____
    a. egg
    b. smelly
    c. fresh
    d. cooked

14. **recipe : chef :: cash register :** _____
    a. money
    b. key
    c. cashier
    d. cash

In this lesson no new types of analogies will be introduced. Instead you will review analogies that you already know how to solve. Remember to study the relationship between the first two words before trying to select the word that completes the second set of words.

1. knight : shield ::
   astronomer : _____
   a. serf
   b. manor
   c. detour
   d. telescope

2. chemist : test tube ::
   accountant : _____
   a. bookkeeper
   b. calculator
   c. curious
   d. accountable

3. trombone : bugle :: lion : _____
   a. fur
   b. pride
   c. cub
   d. tiger

4. strawberry : raspberry ::
   lilac : _____
   a. flower
   b. iris
   c. fragrant
   d. purple

5. jam : blackberry :: silk : _____
   a. dress
   b. smooth
   c. silk worm
   d. rayon

6. apple : apples :: girl : _____
   a. woman
   b. boy
   c. girls
   d. doll

7. judge : supreme court justice ::
   worker : _____
   a. directions
   b. assembly line
   c. foreman
   d. product

8. odometer : distance ::
   altimeter : _____
   a. timid
   b. speed
   c. revolutions
   d. altitude

9. pound : hammer :: pinch : _____
   a. pliers
   b. held
   c. open
   d. pound

10. fasten : pin :: shovel : _____
    a. hoe
    b. spade
    c. sand
    d. hole

11. nephew : niece :: uncle : _____
    a. brother
    b. aunt
    c. grandfather
    d. grandmother

12. lioness : lion :: tigress : _____
    a. cub
    b. striped
    c. tiger
    d. feline

13. fry : fish :: cub : _____
    a. club
    b. small
    c. bear
    d. whimper

14. man : boy :: deer : _____
    a. doe
    b. buck
    c. fawn
    d. hunter

15. Reggae : bluegrass ::
    baroque : _____
    a. abstract
    b. art
    c. painting
    d. Rubens

16. hands : clock ::
    microchip : _____
    a. memory
    b. electronics
    c. computer
    d. mechanics

In this lesson no new types of analogies will be introduced. Instead you will review analogies that you already know how to solve. Remember to think about the relationship between the first two words before trying to select the missing word that completes the second pair of words.

---

**1. eagle : eaglet :: pigeon : _____**
a. fly
b. coop
c. dove
d. squab

**2. kit : muskrat :: owlet : _____**
a. owl
b. baby
c. nest
d. nocturnal

**3. egg : shell :: onion : _____**
a. tears
b. herb
c. scallion
d. skin

**4. hide : cow :: wrapper : _____**
a. gum
b. unwrap
c. fresh
d. paper

**5. tanner : leather ::
glass blower : _____**
a. potter
b. weaver
c. vase
d. shoe

**6. ring : jeweler :: rose : _____**
a. soil
b. cultivate
c. bud
d. gardener

**7. cross : Christianity ::
lion : _____**
a. courage
b. pride
c. lioness
d. cub

**8. addition : + ::
subtraction : _____**
a. math
b. -
c. #
d. =

**9. H$_2$O : water ::
Uncle Sam : _____**
a. stilts
b. hat
c. United States
d. tall

**10. waitress : restaurant ::
bellhop : _____**
a. food
b. bell
c. hotel
d. waiter

**11. airplane : flight attendant ::
football field : _____**
a. stadium
b. quarterback
c. football
d. touchdown

**12. jar : pickle :: jewelry box : _____**
a. open
b. rob
c. necklace
d. lock

**13. paint : can :: ink : _____**
a. black
b. stain
c. pen
d. write

**14. varnish : wood :: polish : _____**
a. shiny
b. wet
c. fingernail
d. sticky

In this lesson no new types of analogies will be introduced. Instead you will review analogies that you already know how to solve. Remember to think about the relationship between the first two words before trying to select the missing word that completes the second pair of words.

1. nail : wood : tape : _____
   a. clear
   b. sticky
   c. paper
   d. tear

2. bread : peanut butter ::
   pancakes : _____
   a. flip
   b. burned
   c. hot cakes
   d. syrup

3. ornothologist : bird ::
   entomologist : _____
   a. insect
   b. epicure
   c. food
   d. chef

4. shale : slate :: limestone : _____
   a. caves
   b. water
   c. chat
   d. marble

5. pearl : oyster :: cider : _____
   a. vinegar
   b. apple
   c. press
   d. quart

6. antithesis : opposite ::
   apothecary : _____
   a. pharmacist
   b. flower
   c. rose
   d. similar

7. astute : shrewd :: odd : _____
   a. even
   b. strange
   c. odds
   d. studious

8. up : down :: east : _____
   a. north
   b. south
   c. eastward
   d. west

9. black : white :: soft : _____
   a. fur
   b. cotton
   c. hard
   d. fluffy

10. wet : dry :: young : _____
    a. new
    b. baby
    c. old
    d. infant

11. kangaroo : pouch ::
    flower : _____
    a. rose
    b. piston
    c. pistil
    d. germinate

12. leaf : plant :: word : _____
    a. speak
    b. sentence
    c. letter
    d. spell

13. holiday : Halloween ::
    religion : _____
    a. pray
    b. minister
    c. Buddhism
    d. Easter

14. nursing : profession ::
    Eiffel Tower : _____
    a. France
    b. tall
    c. landmark
    d. Paris

© 2005 Taylor & Francis- Thinking Through Analogies

This is your chance to write your own analogies. Look at the first two words and think about the relationship between them. Then find two other words with the same relationship that will complete the sentence. Be original and creative!

1. spaghetti : meatball :: _____ : _____

2. pier : pilings :: _____ : _____

3. freeway : expressway :: _____ : _____

4. senior : junior :: _____ : _____

5. goose : gander :: _____ : _____

6. seal : pup :: _____ : _____

7. peacock : peahen :: _____ : _____

8. pen : write :: _____ : _____

9. jacket : book :: _____ : _____

10. ceiling : room :: _____ : _____

11. geese : flock :: _____ : _____

12. paper : pencil :: _____ : _____

13. programmer : software :: _____ : _____

14. nurse : hospital :: _____ : _____

15. seismologist : earthquakes :: _____ : _____

16. seed : plant :: _____ : _____

17. _____ : _____ :: _____ : _____

18. _____ : _____ :: _____ : _____

In this lesson no new types of analogies will be introduced. Instead you will review analogies that you have already learned to solve. Remember to think about the relationship between the first two words before trying to select the missing word that completes the second pair of words.

**1. tool : drill :: language : _____**
a. speak
b. German
c. communicate
d. tongue

**2. cotton : fabric ::**
**hydroelectricity : _____**
a. energy
b. water
c. solar power
d. turbine

**3. company : actor ::**
**college : _____**
a. study
b. student
c. higher
d. ivy

**4. person : family ::**
**tribesman : _____**
a. spear
b. arrow
c. tribe
d. aborigine

**5. uranium : radioactive ::**
**popcorn : _____**
a. pop
b. salt
c. tasty
d. movie

**6. sharp : knife :: red : _____**
a. blue
b. cardinal
c. color
d. read

**7. dentist : drill ::**
**pharmacist : _____**
a. drug store
b. pill counter
c. doctor
d. airplane

**8. camera : photographer ::**
**clothes : _____**
a. dress
b. sew
c. model
d. fashion

**9. silk : satin :: oyster : _____**
a. pearl
b. shell
c. clam
d. ocean

**10. adobe : brick ::**
**California : _____**
a. state
b. gold
c. Pacific
d. Nevada

**11. calf : calves :: dish : _____**
a. plate
b. wash
c. break
d. dishes

**12. teacher : principal ::**
**cowboy : _____**
a. cow
b. trail
c. brand
d. trailboss

**13. director : flutist :: coach : _____**
a. athlete
b. sport
c. important
d. league

**14. meter : kilometer ::**
**apprentice : _____**
a. work
b. learn
c. journeyman
d. hire

In this lesson no new types of analogies will be introduced. Instead you will review analogies that you have already learned to solve. Remember to think about the relationship between the first two words before trying to select the missing word that completes the second pair of words.

**1. child : parent :: pawn : _____**
a. fish
b. little
c. bishop
d. chess

**2. actor : understudy :: doctor : _____**
a. intern
b. medicine
c. wound
d. antiseptic

**3. measuring cup : volume :: test : _____**
a. questions
b. knowledge
c. teacher
d. student

**4. air pressure : tire gauge :: time : _____**
a. minutes
b. clock
c. hours
d. seconds

**5. pain : agony :: costly : _____**
a. cheap
b. money
c. exorbitant
d. bargain

**6. fish hook : bait :: air conditioner : _____**
a. cold
b. run
c. Freon
d. furnace

**7. air mattress : water :: dirigible : _____**
a. float
b. air
c. blimp
d. balloon

**8. hoe : cultivate :: egg beater : _____**
a. egg
b. mix
c. whipped cream
d. cake

**9. scissors : cut :: shovel : _____**
a. loam
b. sand
c. handle
d. dig

**10. mother : father :: wife : _____**
a. child
b. husband
c. son
d. daughter

**11. stallion : mare :: comedian : _____**
a. comedy
b. laughter
c. tragedy
d. commedienne

**12. sundae : cherry :: root beer : _____**
a. drink
b. foam
c. brew
d. barrel

**13. steeple : church :: propeller : _____**
a. helicopter
b. fly
c. runway
d. takeoff

**14. hot dog : casing :: pillow : _____**
a. soft
b. feathers
c. case
d. cushion

In this lesson no new types of analogies will be introduced. Instead you will review analogies that you have already learned to solve. Remember to think about the relationship between the first two words before trying to select the missing word that completes the second pair of words.

1. head : helmet :: patio : _____
   a. outside
   b. cover
   c. canopy
   d. cement

2. pod : pea :: rind : _____
   a. tough
   b. covering
   c. watermelon
   d. seed

3. red and white pole : barber ::
   % : _____
   a. ?
   b. percent
   c. #
   d. "

4. Number : # :: physician : _____
   a. caduceus
   b. operation
   c. hospital
   d. $

5. astronomer : observatory ::
   professor : _____
   a. teach
   b. book
   c. university
   d. learning

6. beach : lifeguard ::
   mountain : _____
   a. snow
   b. Rockies
   c. ski instructor
   d. valleys

7. carton : milk ::
   ice bucket : _____
   a. ice
   b. serve
   c. lid
   d. insulated

8. tea : pitcher ::
   mayonnaise : _____
   a. salad dressing
   b. eggs
   c. jar
   d. blend

9. ivy : wall :: lichens : _____
   a. grown
   b. parasite
   c. boulder
   d. moss

10. anthropologist : mankind ::
    oceanographer : _____
    a. oceans
    b. ships
    c. biologist
    d. mammal

11. wood : charcoal ::
    iron ore : _____
    a. oxygen
    b. rusty
    c. steel
    d. mine

12. glass : sand :: rubber : _____
    a. bounce
    b. ball
    c. hose
    d. latex

13. tiny : small :: lovely : _____
    a. ugly
    b. hideous
    c. pretty
    d. wee

14. bright : dull :: rough : _____
    a. scratch
    b. bumpy
    c. smooth
    d. wet

In this lesson no new types of analogies will be introduced. Instead you will review analogies that you have already learned to solve. Remember to think about the relationship between the first two words before trying to select the missing word that completes the second pair of words.

---

**1. slim : thin :: timid : _____**
a. bold
b. fast
c. shy
d. mouse

**2. bright : dull :: rough : _____**
a. scratchy
b. sandpaper
c. smooth
d. tough

**3. aid : help :: purchase : _____**
a. sell
b. salesman
c. bargain
d. buy

**4. soil : loam :: island : _____**
a. peninsula
b. water
c. isthmus
d. Bermuda

**5. dinghy : boat :: femur : _____**
a. patella
b. tibia
c. humerus
d. bone

**6. armada : ship :: batch : _____**
a. cookie
b. patch
c. boat
d. ocean

**7. baby : little :: path : _____**
a. highway
b. crooked
c. lane
d. driveway

**8. swamp : wet :: desert : _____**
a. bog
b. dry
c. plain
d. Sahara

**9. closet : clothes :: garage : _____**
a. house
b. park
c. car
d. door

**10. script : actor :: balance beam : _____**
a. gymnast
b. trapeze
c. hurdle
d. balance

**11. Nile : Danube :: appaloosa : _____**
a. river
b. horse
c. palomino
d. saddle

**12. pie : pies :: deer : _____**
a. doe
b. buck
c. fawn
d. deer

**13. pawn : bishop :: teller : _____**
a. bank president
b. tell
c. money
d. window

**14. kangaroo : joey :: tree : _____**
a. branch
b. maple
c. root
d. sapling

36

In this lesson no new types of analogies will be introduced. Instead you will review analogies that you have already learned to solve. Remember to think about the relationship between the first two words before trying to select the missing word that completes the second pair of words.

1. twin : triplet :: triplet : _____
   a. three
   b. baby
   c. twin
   d. quadruplet

2. pork : beef :: Cherokee : _____
   a. meat
   b. Indian
   c. Sioux
   d. treaty

3. beverage : tea :: science : _____
   a. biology
   b. study
   c. coffee
   d. scientist

4. attempt : try :: select : _____
   a. shopper
   b. choosy
   c. choose
   d. timely

5. waiter : waitress ::
   groom : _____
   a. broom
   b. bride
   c. horse
   d. food

6. fledgling : bird :: newt : _____
   a. salamander
   b. old
   c. cave
   d. soil

7. sandwich : bread :: book : _____
   a. page
   b. library
   c. cover
   d. volume

8. understudy : actress ::
   plebeian : _____
   a. play
   b. playwright
   c. drama
   d. patrician

9. dulcimer : mandolin ::
   mink : _____
   a. fur
   b. ermine
   c. coat
   d. animal

10. sculpture : art ::
    Kentucky Derby : _____
    a. race
    b. horse
    c. Kentucky
    d. jockey

11. precede : follow ::
    modern : _____
    a. new
    b. spacious
    c. ancient
    d. age

12. widow : widower ::
    grandma : _____
    a. spider
    b. son
    c. grandpa
    d. woman

13. swan : cygnet :: plant : _____
    a. tomato
    b. seedling
    c. root
    d. grow

14. fox : fur :: hand : _____
    a. glove
    b. fist
    c. foot
    d. ball

In this lesson no new types of analogies will be introduced. Instead you will review analogies that you have already learned to solve. Remember to think about the relationship between the first two words before trying to select the missing word that completes the second pair of words.

---

**1. bottle : ketchup :: tube : _____**
a. tub
b. lid
c. toothpaste
d. sticky

**2. botanist : plants :: zoologist : _____**
a. trees
b. animals
c. French
d. zoo

**3. = : equals :: $ : _____**
a. symbol
b. money
c. dollar
d. cent

**4. page : squire :: squire : _____**
a. page
b. squirrel
c. knight
d. tounament

**5. 84 : 14 :: panda : _____**
a. lovable
b. bear
c. fish
d. grizzly

**6. soybeans : crop :: Eli Whitney : _____**
a. corn
b. legume
c. inventor
d. cotton

**7. whitecaps : ocean :: hair : _____**
a. hairdresser
b. head
c. shampoo
d. braids

**8. Farenheit : centigrade :: hovercraft : _____**
a. hydrofoil
b. water
c. air
d. vehicle

**9. languages : linguist :: words : _____**
a. speak
b. write
c. read
d. lexicographer

**10. shaker : salt :: cookie jar : _____**
a. cookie
b. fresh
c. lid
d. pepper

**11. child : parent :: parent : _____**
a. grandparent
b. leader
c. household
d. family

**12. mosquito : flea :: liver : _____**
a. heart
b. bile
c. louse
d. chilly

**13. color : blue :: vehicle : _____**
a. truck
b. locomotion
c. license
d. driver

**14. cactus : spines :: pig : _____**
a. piglet
b. sow
c. bacon
d. bristles

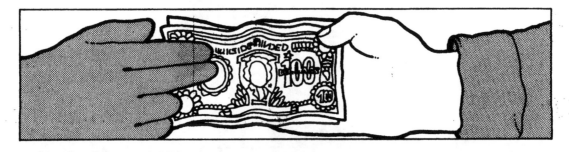

In this lesson no new types of analogies will be introduced. Instead you will review analogies that you have already learned to solve. Remember to think about the relationship between the first two words before trying to select the missing word that completes the second pair of words.

1. **elephant : Republican ::**
   **donkey : _____**
   a. Democratic
   b. democracy
   c. convention
   d. burro

2. **skeleton : orthopedist ::**
   **child : _____**
   a. son
   b. daughter
   c. pediatrician
   d. youngster

3. **sport : soccer :: game : _____**
   a. fun
   b. chess
   c. player
   d. pawn

4. **clothes : body :: shoe : _____**
   a. polish
   b. boot
   c. foot
   d. leather

5. **cooper : barrel ::**
   **blacksmith : _____**
   a. stave
   b. fire
   c. muscular
   d. horseshoe

6. **black : mourning ::**
   **red cross : _____**
   a. medical aid
   b. happy
   c. eliminate
   d. hatred

7. **Appalachians : Rockies ::**
   **Atlantic : _____**
   a. mountain
   b. ocean
   c. Pacific
   d. coast

8. **penny : luck :: × : _____**
   a. extra
   b. multiplication
   c. welcome
   d. nickle

9. **skirmish : battle :: battle : _____**
   a. war
   b. soldier
   c. bomb
   d. weapon

10. **pear : fruit :: cheddar : _____**
    a. Swiss
    b. cheese
    c. milk
    d. ferment

11. **wool : sheep :: quills : _____**
    a. lamb
    b. mutton
    c. sharp
    d. porcupine

12. **NE : northeast :: SW : _____**
    a. west
    b. southwest
    c. east
    d. downhill

13. **cent : ¢ :: division : _____**
    a. &
    b. multiplication
    c. subtraction
    d. ÷

14. **slipper : ballerina ::**
    **boots : _____**
    a. cowboy
    b. dance
    c. pair
    d. moccasins

# Answers

**Lesson 1 - pg. 4**
| | |
|---|---|
| 1. c | 8. d |
| 2. a | 9. c |
| 3. c | 10. a |
| 4. b | 11. d |
| 5. c | 12. c |
| 6. a | 13. d |
| 7. d | 14. d |

**Lesson 2 - pg. 5**
| | |
|---|---|
| 1. b | 8. a |
| 2. d | 9. c |
| 3. a | 10. c |
| 4. d | 11. c |
| 5. a | 12. b |
| 6. d | 13. a |
| 7. b | 14. d |

**Lesson 3 - pg. 6**
| | |
|---|---|
| 1. c | 8. c |
| 2. a | 9. a |
| 3. d | 10. c |
| 4. d | 11. c |
| 5. b | 12. d |
| 6. c | 13. c |
| 7. d | 14. a |

**Lesson 4 - pg. 7**
| | |
|---|---|
| 1. b | 8. c |
| 2. c | 9. c |
| 3. d | 10. b |
| 4. a | 11. a |
| 5. c | 12. c |
| 6. b | 13. c |
| 7. b | 14. b |

**Review Lesson 1 - pg. 8**
| | |
|---|---|
| 1. c | 8. c |
| 2. a | 9. c |
| 3. d | 10. d |
| 4. b | 11. d |
| 5. a | 12. a |
| 6. d | 13. b |
| 7. a | 14. c |

**Pot Pourri Lesson 1 - pg. 9**
| | |
|---|---|
| 1. a | 7. e |
| 2. b | 8. e |
| 3. a | 9. c |
| 4. c | 10. d |
| 5. b | 11. b |
| 6. a | 12. a |

**Lesson 5 - pg. 11**
| | |
|---|---|
| 1. b | 8. b |
| 2. c | 9. c |
| 3. d | 10. c |
| 4. c | 11. a |
| 5. b | 12. b |
| 6. d | 13. c |
| 7. a | 14. d |

**Lesson 6 - pg. 12**
| | |
|---|---|
| 1. c | 8. b |
| 2. b | 9. d |
| 3. c | 10. a |
| 4. b | 11. c |
| 5. d | 12. d |
| 6. b | 13. b |
| 7. a | 14. d |

**Lesson 7 - pg. 13**
| | |
|---|---|
| 1. b | 8. a |
| 2. c | 9. c |
| 3. a | 10. b |
| 4. b | 11. c |
| 5. d | 12. a |
| 6. c | 13. b |
| 7. b | 14. a |

**Lesson 8 -pg. 14**
| | |
|---|---|
| 1. b | 8. a |
| 2. a | 9. c |
| 3. b | 10. a |
| 4. c | 11. d |
| 5. b | 12. c |
| 6. a | 13. b |
| 7. b | 14. c |

**Review Lesson 2 - pg. 15**
| | |
|---|---|
| 1. b | 8. d |
| 2. a | 9. d |
| 3. c | 10. b |
| 4. b | 11. d |
| 5. c | 12. c |
| 6. b | 13. c |
| 7. d | 14. a |

**Review Lesson 3 - pg. 16**
| | |
|---|---|
| 1. b | 8. d |
| 2. c | 9. c |
| 3. a | 10. a |
| 4. b | 11. d |
| 5. c | 12. b |
| 6. d | 13. a |
| 7. c | 14. c |

**Pot Pourri Lesson 2 - pg. 17**
| | |
|---|---|
| 1. a | 7. c |
| 2. b | 8. c |
| 3. b | 9. e |
| 4. d | 10. e |
| 5. c | 11. f |
| 6. a | 12. c |

**Lesson 9 - pg. 19**
| | |
|---|---|
| 1. c | 8. a |
| 2. b | 9. c |
| 3. d | 10. b |
| 4. c | 11. b |
| 5. a | 12. d |
| 6. b | 13. a |
| 7. c | 14. d |

**Lesson 10 - pg. 20**
| | |
|---|---|
| 1. b | 8. c |
| 2. d | 9. c |
| 3. a | 10. d |
| 4. c | 11. d |
| 5. d | 12. d |
| 6. d | 13. b |
| 7. a | 14. c |

**Lesson 11 - pg. 21**
| | |
|---|---|
| 1. d | 8. d |
| 2. c | 9. b |
| 3. a | 10. c |
| 4. c | 11. c |
| 5. d | 12. d |
| 6. b | 13. c |
| 7. d | 14. a |

**Lesson 12 - pg. 22**
| | |
|---|---|
| 1. b. | 8. c |
| 2. a | 9. b |
| 3. c | 10. a |
| 4. d | 11. d |
| 5. c | 12. d |
| 6. d | 13. c |
| 7. c | 14. c |

**Lesson 13 - pg. 23**
| | |
|---|---|
| 1. b | 8. c |
| 2. d | 9. b |
| 3. c | 10. c |
| 4. d | 11. d |
| 5. d | 12. d |
| 6. b | 13. b |
| 7. d | 14. d |

**Review Lesson 4 - pg. 24**
| | |
|---|---|
| 1. c | 8. a |
| 2. a | 9. b |
| 3. c | 10. b |
| 4. a | 11. d |
| 5. d | 12. d |
| 6. b | 13. c |
| 7. b | 14. b |

**Review Lesson 5 - pg. 25**
| | |
|---|---|
| 1. c. | 8. c |
| 2. a. | 9. d |
| 3. d | 10. b |
| 4. c | 11. c |
| 5. d | 12. c |
| 6. b | 13. c |
| 7. b | 14. d |

**Review Lesson 6 - pg. 26**
| | |
|---|---|
| 1. c | 8. c |
| 2. c | 9. c |
| 3. b | 10. d |
| 4. a | 11. d |
| 5. d | 12. c |
| 6. c | 13. b |
| 7. b | 14. c |

**Review Lesson 7 - pg. 28**
| | |
|---|---|
| 1. c | 8. b |
| 2. a | 9. c |
| 3. c | 10. d |
| 4. d | 11. d |
| 5. b | 12. a |
| 6. c | 13. a |
| 7. a | 14. c |

**Review Lesson 8 - pg. 29**
| | |
|---|---|
| 1. d | 9. a |
| 2. b | 10. b |
| 3. d | 11. b |
| 4. b | 12. c |
| 5. c | 13. c |
| 6. c | 14. c |
| 7. c | 15. a |
| 8. d | 16. c |

**Review Lesson 9** - pg. 30

| | |
|---|---|
| 1. d | 8. b |
| 2. a | 9. c |
| 3. d | 10. c |
| 4. a | 11. b |
| 5. c | 12. c |
| 6. d | 13. c |
| 7. a | 14. c |

**Review Lesson 10** - pg. 31

| | |
|---|---|
| 1. c | 8. d |
| 2. d | 9. c |
| 3. a | 10. c |
| 4. d | 11. c |
| 5. b | 12. b |
| 6. a | 13. c |
| 7. b | 14. c |

**Review Lesson 11** - pg. 33

| | |
|---|---|
| 1. b | 8. c |
| 2. a | 9. c |
| 3. b | 10. d |
| 4. c | 11. d |
| 5. c | 12. d |
| 6. b | 13. a |
| 7. b | 14. c |

**Review Lesson 12** - pg. 34

| | |
|---|---|
| 1. c | 8. b |
| 2. a | 9. d |
| 3. b | 10. b |
| 4. b | 11. d |
| 5. c | 12. b |
| 6. c | 13. a |
| 7. b | 14. c |

**Review Lesson 13** - pg. 35

| | |
|---|---|
| 1. c | 8. c |
| 2. c | 9. c |
| 3. b | 10. a |
| 4. a | 11. c |
| 5. c | 12. d |
| 6. c | 13. c |
| 7. a | 14. c |

**Review Lesson 14** - pg. 36

| | |
|---|---|
| 1. c | 8. b |
| 2. c | 9. c |
| 3. d | 10. a |
| 4. d | 11. c |
| 5. d | 12. d |
| 6. a | 13. a |
| 7. b | 14. d |

**Review Lesson 15** - pg. 37

| | |
|---|---|
| 1. d | 8. d |
| 2. c | 9. b |
| 3. a | 10. a |
| 4. c | 11. c |
| 5. b | 12. c |
| 6. a | 13. b |
| 7. c | 14. a |

**Review Lesson 16** - pg. 38

| | |
|---|---|
| 1. c | 8. a |
| 2. b | 9. d |
| 3. c | 10. a |
| 4. c | 11. a |
| 5. d | 12. a |
| 6. c | 13. a |
| 7. b | 14. d |

**Review Lesson 17** - pg. 39

| | |
|---|---|
| 1. a | 8. b |
| 2. c | 9. a |
| 3. b | 10. b |
| 4. c | 11. d |
| 5. d | 12. b |
| 6. a | 13. d |
| 7. c | 14. a |

Printed in the United States
by Baker & Taylor Publisher Services